contents

British & North American Readers:
Please note that Australian cup and spoon measurements are metric. A quick conversion guide appears on page 63. A glossary explaining unfamiliar terms and ingredients begins on page 61.

2 let's jam!

By following these tried-and-tested procedures, your jams and jellies will be a guaranteed triumph – sweet, delicious and simple.

First things first

Jam is based on one or more types of fruit. The fruit is cooked until tender, sugar is added, then the mixture is cooked until it will jell, or become thick enough to spread when it is served at room temperature. A conserve is a preserve made from whole or large pieces of fruit, made in the same way as jam.

A jelly differs from jam in that it is made using only the strained juice from the cooked fruit (the fruit pulp is discarded). The juice is combined with sugar then cooked to a point at which it will set at room temperature. A good jelly should be transparent, firm enough to hold its own shape, but soft enough to quiver when cut with a spoon.

To test if jam/jelly has jelled

When your jam or jelly is thickening – at this stage, the mixture will have reduced to about half the original quantity – remove it from heat to test if it has jelled. Drop a teaspoon of mixture onto a saucer that has been chilled in a freezer for a few minutes. Return saucer to freezer until jam or jelly has cooled.

• Jam that contains pieces of fruit should have formed a skin that wrinkles when pushed with finger.

Push jam with a finger to test if it has jelled

• Jam that has a thick and pulpy texture should have a spreadable consistency.

• Jelly should be a firm mass on the saucer. If mixture has not jelled, return to heat and boil mixture rapidly until it will jell when subsequently tested (this may only take a few minutes).

If you have a candy thermometer, it's handy to know that jams and jellies will reach jelling point at 105°C to 106°C.

Straining fruit to make jelly

Cooked fruit must be strained through damp muslin or other fine cloth to make jelly, following either of these easy methods.

• A cone-shaped jelly bag, with attachments for hanging, can be purchased from specialist kitchen stores; dampen the bag before use.

A homemade jelly bag will work just as well

• A jelly bag can be made by tying the corners of a square of damp, fine cloth (muslin, boiled unbleached calico, sheet) to the legs of an upturned chair or stool, leaving cloth loose enough to dip in the centre. Place a large bowl under the bag or cloth. Pour the fruit and its liquid into the bag or cloth; allow mixture to drip through bag/cloth for several hours or overnight. Do not squeeze or press the mixture through the bag/cloth as this will result in cloudy jelly.

Pectin content in jelly

Each jelly recipe requires you to test the strained juice for pectin content to determine how much sugar to add. This differs based on ripeness, acidity and type of fruit used.

To test for pectin content: Place 1 teaspoon strained fruit liquid in a glass, add 3 teaspoons methylated spirits; stir mixture gently. The liquid is normally almost colourless; we added colour to our fruit liquid so it could be seen in the photograph.

• If mixture forms fairly solid, single jelly-like clot, the fruit liquid is high in pectin; in this case use 1 cup (220g) sugar per 1 cup fruit liquid.

• If several smaller clots of jelly form, the jelly is not high in pectin; use 3/4 cup (165g) sugar per 1 cup fruit liquid.

Here, the mixture forms a single solid jelly-like clot

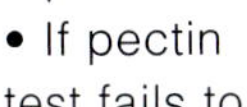

• If pectin test fails to produce any clots, or gives a mass of tiny clots, add some fruit juice naturally rich in pectin – usually 2 tablespoons fresh strained lemon juice per 1kg fruit used; add this after sugar has dissolved.

Please turn to page 60 for further essential jam-making information.

4 fruit salad jam

You will need three large bananas and about three passionfruit for this recipe.

1⅔ cups (250g) dried apricots

2 cups (500ml) water

1 cup (250ml) undrained crushed pineapple in syrup

½ cup (125ml) fresh orange juice

¼ cup (60ml) passionfruit pulp

3 cups (660g) sugar

2 cups sliced bananas

Combine apricots and the water in medium bowl; cover, stand 3 hours or overnight.

Combine undrained apricots with pineapple in large saucepan; simmer, covered, 15 minutes. Add juice and passionfruit pulp, bring to a boil; reduce heat, simmer, covered, 10 minutes. Add sugar; stir over heat, without boiling, until sugar dissolves. Add banana; boil, uncovered, stirring occasionally, about 20 minutes or until jam jells when tested. Stand 5 minutes. Pour hot jam into hot sterilised jars; seal while hot.

MAKES about 1.5 litres (6 cups)

Per tablespoon 0g fat; 209kJ

6 cumquat

ginger marmalade

1kg cumquats

1.75 litres (7 cups) water

1.5kg (7 cups) sugar

1 tablespoon grated fresh ginger

Slice cumquats thinly; remove seeds, reserve. Put seeds and 1 cup (250ml) of the water in small bowl; cover, set aside. Combine sliced cumquats in large bowl with remaining water. Stand both cumquat mixture and seeds, separately, overnight.

Next day, drain seeds over small bowl; reserve liquid, discard seeds. Combine cumquat mixture and reserved liquid in large saucepan; bring to a boil. Reduce heat; simmer, covered, about 30 minutes or until cumquats are tender. Add sugar; stir over heat, without boiling, until sugar dissolves.

Boil, uncovered, stirring occasionally, about 15 minutes or until marmalade jells when tested. Stir in ginger; stand 5 minutes. Pour hot marmalade into hot sterilised jars; seal while hot.

MAKES about 1.75 litres (7 cups)
Per tablespoon 0g fat; 304kJ

apple passionfruit jelly

You will need about six passionfruit for this recipe.

5 large apples (1kg)

1.5 litres (6 cups) water

1kg (4½ cups) sugar, approximately

½ cup (125ml) passionfruit pulp

Cut unpeeled apples crossways into thin slices. Combine apples (including seeds and cores) with the water in large saucepan; bring to a boil. Reduce heat; simmer, covered, 1 hour. Strain mixture through large piece of damp muslin into large bowl; allow mixture to drip through cloth for several hours or overnight. Do not squeeze or press the mixture through the cloth as this will result in cloudy jelly.

Measure the strained liquid, discard pulp. Allow the correct amount of sugar (according to pectin test, page 3) to each cup of liquid. Return liquid with sugar to clean large saucepan; stir over heat, without boiling, until sugar dissolves. Boil, uncovered, without stirring, about 15 minutes or until jelly sets when tested. Gently stir passionfruit pulp through jelly; stand 5 minutes. Pour hot jelly into hot sterilised jars; seal while hot.

MAKES about 3½ cups (875ml)

Per tablespoon 0g fat; 421kJ

8 tomato, lemon and port marmalade

5 medium lemons (700g)

3½ cups (875ml) water

4 cups (880g) sugar, approximately

6 large tomatoes (1.5kg), peeled, chopped coarsely

1 cup (220g) sugar, extra

½ cup (125ml) port

Cut unpeeled lemons into 5mm slices. Remove seeds, tie seeds in piece of muslin. Place lemon slices, muslin bag and the water in large bowl; cover, stand overnight.

Next day, transfer lemon mixture to large saucepan; bring to a boil. Reduce heat; simmer, covered, stirring occasionally, about 1 hour or until rind is soft. Discard muslin bag.

Measure fruit mixture, allow 1 cup (220g) sugar to each cup of fruit mixture. Return fruit mixture and sugar to pan with tomato and extra sugar. Stir over heat, without boiling, until sugar dissolves. Boil, uncovered, stirring occasionally, about 40 minutes or until mixture is reduced by half. Stir in port; boil, uncovered, about 5 minutes or until marmalade jells when tested.

Pour hot marmalade into hot sterilised jars; seal while hot.

MAKES about 1.5 litres (6 cups)

Per tablespoon 0g fat; 276kJ

green tomato jam

1 small orange (180g), halved

1 medium lemon (140g), halved

1/4 cup (60ml) water

4 large green tomatoes (1kg), sliced thinly

3 cups (660g) sugar

1/4 cup (55g) glacé ginger, sliced thinly

Remove seeds from citrus fruit; tie seeds in piece of muslin. Blend or process unpeeled citrus fruit and the water until finely chopped.
Combine citrus mixture with tomato in large saucepan; bring to a boil. Reduce heat; simmer, uncovered, stirring occasionally, about 10 minutes or until tomato is pulpy. Add muslin bag and remaining ingredients to pan; stir over heat, without boiling, until sugar dissolves. Boil, uncovered, stirring occasionally, about 30 minutes or until jam jells when tested.
Discard muslin bag. Pour hot jam into hot sterilised jars; seal while hot.

MAKES about 1.25 litres (5 cups)
Per tablespoon 0g fat; 205kJ

10 grapefruit and brandy marmalade

3 large grapefruit (1.5kg)
1 litre (4 cups) water
1.3kg (6 cups) sugar
1/3 cup (80ml) brandy

Coarsely chop unpeeled grapefruit, seeds and all; process until mixture is chopped finely.

Combine grapefruit mixture and the water in large saucepan; bring to a boil. Reduce heat; simmer, covered, 30 minutes. Transfer mixture to large bowl, cover; stand overnight.

Return fruit mixture to pan with sugar; stir over heat, without boiling, until sugar dissolves. Boil, uncovered, stirring occasionally, about 20 minutes or until marmalade jells when tested. Stir in brandy, stand 5 minutes. Pour hot marmalade into hot sterilised jars; seal while hot.

MAKES about 2 litres (8 cups)
Per tablespoon 0g fat; 241kJ

rhubarb and carrot conserve

4 medium (500g) carrots, chopped coarsely

500g rhubarb, chopped coarsely

1 teaspoon finely grated lemon rind

2 tablespoons fresh lemon juice

1 litre (4 cups) water

4½ cups (1kg) sugar

¼ cup (55g) glacé ginger, chopped finely

Combine carrot, rhubarb, rind, juice and the water in large saucepan; bring to a boil. Reduce heat; simmer, covered, 15 minutes or until carrot is soft. **Stir** in sugar and ginger; stir over heat, without boiling, until sugar dissolves. Boil, uncovered, stirring occasionally, about 15 minutes or until conserve jells when tested. Pour hot conserve into hot sterilised jars; seal while hot.

MAKES about 1 litre (4 cups)
Per tablespoon 0g fat; 383kJ

12 lime and fig marmalade

10 large limes (1kg)

2 litres (8 cups) water

1.3kg (6 cups) sugar, approximately

1¼ cups (240g) dried figs, sliced thinly

Remove rind from limes, cut rind into thin strips. Remove and reserve pith from limes; chop lime flesh coarsely, reserve seeds. Tie pith and seeds in piece of muslin. Combine rind, lime flesh, muslin bag and the water in large saucepan; bring to a boil. Reduce heat; simmer, covered, about 1 hour or until rind is soft. Discard muslin bag.

Measure fruit mixture, allow ¾ cup (165g) sugar to each cup of fruit mixture. Return fruit mixture with sugar to pan; stir over heat, without boiling, until sugar dissolves. Boil, uncovered, stirring occasionally, about 35 minutes or until marmalade jells when tested. Stir in figs. Pour hot marmalade into hot sterilised jars; seal while hot.

MAKES about 1.75 litres (7 cups)

Per tablespoon 0g fat; 287kJ

lemon and coconut marmalade

8 medium lemons (1.1kg)

2 litres (8 cups) water

1.8kg (8 cups) sugar, approximately

1 cup (50g) flaked coconut, toasted

Cut unpeeled lemons in half lengthways; cut halves into thin slices, reserve seeds. Tie reserved lemon seeds in piece of muslin. Combine lemon slices, the water and muslin bag in large bowl; cover, stand overnight.

Transfer fruit mixture to large saucepan; bring to a boil. Reduce heat; simmer, covered, about 30 minutes or until rind is soft. Discard muslin bag.

Measure fruit mixture, allow 1 cup (220g) sugar to each cup of fruit mixture. Return fruit mixture with sugar to pan; stir over heat, without boiling, until sugar dissolves. Boil, uncovered, stirring occasionally, about 45 minutes or until marmalade jells when tested. Stir in coconut.

Pour hot marmalade into hot sterilised jars; seal while hot.

MAKES about 2 litres (8 cups)

Per tablespoon 0.4g fat; 325kJ

14 orange and passionfruit jelly marmalade

You will need about six passionfruit for this recipe.

8 medium oranges (1.9kg)

1/2 cup (125ml) water

4 medium lemons (560g)

3 litres (12 cups) water, extra

1.4kg (6 1/2 cups) sugar, approximately

1/2 cup (125ml) passionfruit pulp

Using a zester, remove rind from two of the oranges, cover rind with the water; cover, stand 3 hours.

Meanwhile, coarsely chop the two zested oranges, remaining oranges and lemons. Combine fruits, including seeds and rind (but excluding the soaking orange rind), in large saucepan with the extra water; bring to a boil. Reduce heat; simmer, covered, about 1 hour or until rind is soft. Strain mixture through large piece of damp muslin into large bowl; allow mixture to drip through cloth for several hours or overnight. Do not squeeze or press the mixture through the cloth as this will result in cloudy jelly.

Measure the strained liquid, discard pulp. Allow 3/4 cup (165g) sugar to each cup of liquid. Return liquid with sugar and drained orange rind to clean large saucepan; stir over heat, without boiling, until sugar dissolves. Boil, uncovered, without stirring, about 45 minutes or until marmalade jells when tested. Stir in passionfruit pulp; stand 5 minutes. Pour hot marmalade into hot sterilised jars; seal while hot.

MAKES about 1.75 litres (7 cups)

Per tablespoon 0g fat; 311kJ

16 grape and sherry jelly

1kg white grapes, crushed

1 medium lemon (140g), sliced thinly

2 large apples (400g), chopped coarsely

½ cup (125ml) sweet white wine

¾ cup (180ml) water

1 cinnamon stick

4 cardamom seeds, crushed

1¾ cups (385g) sugar, approximately

2 tablespoons sweet sherry

Combine grapes, lemon and apple (including seeds and cores) with wine, the water, cinnamon and cardamom in large saucepan; bring to a boil. Reduce heat; simmer, covered, 1 hour.

Strain mixture through large piece of damp muslin into large bowl; allow mixture to drip through cloth for several hours or overnight. Do not squeeze or press the mixture through the cloth as this will result in cloudy jelly.

Measure the strained liquid, discard pulp. Allow the correct amount of sugar (according to pectin test, page 3) to each cup of liquid. Return liquid with sugar to clean large saucepan; stir over heat, without boiling, until sugar dissolves. Boil, uncovered, without stirring, about 10 minutes or until jelly sets when tested. Stir in sherry. Pour hot jelly into hot sterilised jars; seal while hot.

MAKES about 2 cups (500ml)

Per tablespoon 0.1g fat; 420kJ

sugar-free pear and blueberry jam

500g blueberries

2 small pears (300g), peeled, chopped coarsely

2 tablespoons fresh lemon juice

2 teaspoons white vinegar

2 teaspoons liquid sweetener

2 tablespoons Jamsetta

½ teaspoon tartaric acid

Combine blueberries, pear, juice and vinegar in large saucepan; bring to a boil. Reduce heat; simmer, covered, about 25 minutes or until fruit is soft. **Stir** in remaining ingredients; boil, uncovered, stirring occasionally, about 5 minutes or until jam jells when tested. Pour hot jam into hot sterilised jars; seal while hot.

MAKES about 1½ cups (375ml)
Per tablespoon 0g fat; 110kJ

18 apricot lemon marmalade

1 large orange (300g)

2 large lemons (360g)

2 tablespoons water

1⅔ cups (250g) dried apricots

1.75 litres (7 cups) water, extra

2kg (9 cups) sugar, approximately

Remove and reserve seeds from unpeeled quartered orange and lemons. Put seeds and the 2 tablespoons of water in small bowl, cover; set aside. Blend or process chopped orange, lemons and apricots, in batches, until finely chopped.

Combine fruit mixture with the extra water in large saucepan; bring to a boil. Reduce heat; simmer, covered, 45 minutes. Transfer mixture to large heatproof bowl, cover. Stand fruit mixture and seed mixture, separately, overnight.

Drain seeds over small bowl; reserve liquid, discard seeds. Measure fruit mixture; allow 1 cup (220g) sugar to each cup of fruit mixture. Return fruit mixture with reserved seed liquid to pan; bring to a boil. Add sugar; stir over heat, without boiling, until sugar dissolves. Boil, uncovered, stirring occasionally, about 30 minutes or until marmalade jells when tested. Stand 5 minutes. Pour hot marmalade into hot sterilised jars; seal while hot.

MAKES about 2 litres (8 cups)

Per tablespoon 0g fat; 363kJ

20 strawberry jam

1kg strawberries, quartered

$5\frac{1}{4}$ cups (1.1kg) sugar

$\frac{1}{3}$ cup (80ml) water

$\frac{1}{2}$ cup (125ml) fresh lemon juice

$\frac{1}{4}$ cup (60ml) Grand Marnier

Combine strawberries, sugar, the water and juice in large saucepan; stir over heat, without boiling, until sugar dissolves. Boil, uncovered, stirring occasionally, about 20 minutes or until jam jells when tested. Stir in liqueur. Pour hot jam into hot sterilised jars; seal while hot.

MAKES about 1 litre (4 cups)
Per tablespoon 0g fat; 409kJ

apple and rosé jelly

5 large apples (1kg)

1 medium lemon (140g)

1.5 litres (6 cups) water

1 cup (250ml) rosé wine

1.5kg (7 cups) sugar, approximately

Chop unpeeled apples and lemon coarsely. Combine chopped fruit (including seeds and cores) with the water in large saucepan; bring to a boil. Reduce heat; simmer, covered, about 1 hour or until fruit is pulpy. Add wine; simmer, covered, 30 minutes. Strain mixture through large piece of damp muslin into large bowl; allow mixture to drip through cloth for several hours or overnight. Do not squeeze or press the mixture through the cloth as this will result in cloudy jelly.

Measure the strained liquid, discard pulp. Allow the correct amount of sugar (according to pectin test, page 3) to each cup of liquid. Return liquid with sugar to clean large saucepan; stir over heat, without boiling, until sugar dissolves. Boil, uncovered, without stirring, about 10 minutes or until jelly sets when tested. Pour hot jelly into hot sterilised jars; seal while hot.

MAKES about 1.5 litres (6 cups)

Per tablespoon 0g fat; 366kJ

22 whisky seville marmalade

4 medium Seville oranges (1kg)

2 litres (8 cups) water

2.4kg (11 cups) sugar, approximately

1/4 cup (60ml) whisky

Slice unpeeled oranges very thinly; reserve seeds. Put seeds and 1 cup (250ml) of the water in small bowl; cover, set aside. Place sliced fruit in large bowl with remaining water. Stand both fruit mixture and seeds, separately, overnight.

Drain seeds over small bowl; reserve liquid, discard seeds. Combine fruit mixture and seed liquid in large saucepan; bring to a boil. Reduce heat; simmer, covered, about 1 hour or until rind is tender.

Measure fruit mixture, allow 1 cup (220g) sugar to each cup of fruit mixture. Return fruit mixture with sugar to pan; stir over heat, without boiling, until sugar dissolves. Boil, uncovered, stirring occasionally, about 30 minutes or until marmalade jells when tested. Stand 5 minutes, stir in whisky. Pour hot marmalade into hot sterilised jars; seal while hot.

MAKES about 2.5 litres (10 cups)

Per tablespoon 0g fat; 337kJ

24 dried apricot jam

3⅓ cups (500g) dried apricots, chopped coarsely

1.25 litres (5 cups) water

1kg (4½ cups) sugar

¼ cup (60ml) fresh lemon juice

Combine apricots and the water in large bowl; cover, stand overnight. **Transfer** apricot mixture with sugar and juice to large saucepan; stir over heat, without boiling, until sugar dissolves. Boil, uncovered, stirring occasionally, about 25 minutes or until jam jells when tested. Pour hot jam into hot sterilised jars; seal while hot.

MAKES about 1.5 litres (6 cups)

Per tablespoon 0g fat; 229kJ

25

dried peach, apple and brandy jam

$1\frac{3}{4}$ cups (150g) dried apples, chopped coarsely

$2\frac{2}{3}$ cups (400g) coarsely chopped dried peaches

1.25 litres (5 cups) water

1kg ($4\frac{1}{2}$ cups) sugar

$\frac{1}{4}$ cup (60ml) fresh lemon juice

2 tablespoons brandy

Combine fruit and the water in large bowl; cover, stand overnight. **Transfer** fruit mixture with sugar and juice to large saucepan; stir over heat, without boiling, until sugar dissolves. Boil, uncovered, stirring occasionally, about 25 minutes or until jam jells when tested. Remove pan from heat; stir in brandy. Pour hot jam into hot sterilised jars; seal while hot.

MAKES about 1.5 litres (6 cups)

Per tablespoon 0.1g fat; 293kJ

26 apricot

amaretto jam

1 2/3 cups (250g) dried apricots, sliced thinly

1 1/2 cups (375ml) water

2 teaspoons finely grated orange rind

1 cup (250ml) fresh orange juice

2 tablespoons fresh lemon juice

1 1/4 cups (275g) sugar

1/2 cup (70g) slivered almonds

2 tablespoons Amaretto

Place apricots and the water in medium bowl; cover, stand overnight.
Combine apricot mixture and rind in large saucepan; bring to a boil. Reduce heat; simmer, uncovered, about 10 minutes or until apricots are soft. Add juices and sugar; stir over heat, without boiling, until sugar dissolves.
Boil, uncovered, stirring occasionally, about 30 minutes or until jam jells when tested. Stir in almonds and liqueur. Pour hot jam into hot sterilised jars; seal while hot.

MAKES about 2 1/2 cups (625ml)
Per tablespoon 1.3g fat; 310kJ

28 mixed berry jam

400g frozen raspberries

300g frozen blackberries

300g frozen blueberries

2 cups (500ml) water

½ cup (125ml) fresh lemon juice

4 cups (880g) sugar

Combine berries with the water and juice in large saucepan; bring to a boil. Reduce heat; simmer, uncovered, 20 minutes. Add sugar; stir over heat, without boiling, until sugar dissolves. **Boil**, uncovered, stirring occasionally, about 15 minutes or until jam jells when tested. Pour hot jam into hot sterilised jars; seal while hot.

MAKES about 1.5 litres (6 cups)
Per tablespoon
0g fat; 221kJ

rhubarb and apple jam

4 cups (500g) finely chopped rhubarb

5 large apples (1kg), peeled, sliced thinly

1/2 cup (125ml) water

1/2 cup (125ml) fresh lemon juice

1kg (4 1/2 cups) sugar, approximately

Combine rhubarb, apple, the water and juice in large saucepan; bring to a boil. Reduce heat; simmer, covered, about 20 minutes or until fruit is pulpy. **Measure** fruit mixture, allow 3/4 cup (165g) sugar to each cup of fruit mixture. Return fruit mixture with sugar to pan; stir over heat, without boiling, until sugar dissolves. Boil, uncovered, stirring occasionally, about 10 minutes or until jam sets to a spreading consistency when tested. Pour hot jam into hot sterilised jars; seal while hot.

MAKES about 1.5 litres (6 cups)
Per tablespoon 0g fat; 248kJ

30

pineapple and citrus fruit marmalade

2 medium grapefruit (850g)

2 medium limes (160g)

2 medium oranges (480g)

1 litre (4 cups) water

1 small pineapple (800g), peeled, chopped finely

1.3kg (6 cups) sugar, approximately

2 tablespoons fresh lime juice

Peel rind thinly from grapefruit, limes and oranges, avoiding white pith. Cut rind into thin strips. Remove and discard pith from citrus fruit; reserve seeds, tie in piece of muslin. Chop citrus flesh finely. Combine rind, muslin bag, citrus flesh and the water in large bowl; cover, stand overnight.

Transfer fruit mixture to large saucepan, add pineapple; bring to a boil. Reduce heat; simmer, covered, about 45 minutes or until rind is very tender. Discard muslin bag.

Measure fruit mixture, allow 1 cup (220g) sugar to each cup of fruit mixture. Return fruit mixture with sugar to pan; stir over heat, without boiling, until sugar dissolves.

Add juice; boil, uncovered, stirring occasionally, about 35 minutes or until marmalade jells when tested. Stand 5 minutes. Pour hot marmalade into hot sterilised jars; seal while hot.

MAKES about 1.25 litres (5 cups)

Per tablespoon 0.1g fat; 389kJ

32 microwave jams

The colour and flavour of jams cooked in a microwave oven is excellent, and these mouth-watering recipes will attest to that. When microwaving jams, always use a large, shallow microwave-safe container and remember to follow the golden rule: check the preserve often during cooking time. These recipes have been tested in a 900-watt microwave oven.

tomato jam

4 medium tomatoes (750g), peeled

1 small apple (130g), peeled, grated coarsely

1/3 cup (65g) finely chopped glacé ginger

1/4 cup (60ml) fresh lemon juice

2 cups (440g) caster sugar

Coarsely chop tomatoes, combine with apple and ginger in large glass microwave-safe bowl; cook, uncovered, on HIGH (100%) about 15 minutes or until mixture is pulpy. Add juice and sugar; stir until sugar dissolves. **Cook**, uncovered, on HIGH (100%) about 20 minutes or until jam jells when tested, stirring three times during cooking. Pour hot jam into hot sterilised jars; seal while hot.

MAKES about 1 litre (4 cups)
Per tablespoon 0g fat; 179kJ

apricot and passionfruit jam

You will need about six passionfruit for this recipe.

3 1/3 cups (500g) dried apricots, halved

1/4 cup (60ml) fresh lemon juice

2 cups (500ml) water

4 cups (880g) caster sugar

1/2 cup (125ml) passionfruit pulp

Combine apricots, juice and the water in large glass microwave-safe bowl; cook, uncovered, on HIGH (100%) 15 minutes, stirring once during cooking. Add sugar; stir until sugar dissolves. **Cook**, uncovered, on HIGH (100%) about 10 minutes or until jam jells when tested, stirring three times during cooking. Add passionfruit pulp; stand 2 minutes, stir jam to distribute seeds. Pour hot jam into hot sterilised jars; seal while hot.

MAKES about 1.25 litres (5 cups)
Per tablespoon 0g fat; 308kJ

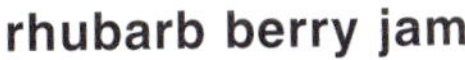

rhubarb berry jam

4 cups (440g) coarsely chopped rhubarb

500g fresh or frozen blackberries

1 teaspoon finely grated orange rind

1 tablespoon fresh orange juice

1 tablespoon fresh lemon juice

1¾ cups (385g) caster sugar

Combine rhubarb, berries, rind and juices in large glass microwave-safe bowl; cook, uncovered, on HIGH (100%) 10 minutes, stirring once during cooking. Add sugar; stir until sugar dissolves.

Cook, uncovered, on HIGH (100%) about 20 minutes or until jam jells when tested, stirring three times during cooking. Pour hot jam into hot sterilised jars; seal while hot.

MAKES about 3 cups (750ml)

Per tablespoon 0.1g fat; 221kJ

34 easy mixed-fruit jam

2 medium lemons (280g)

1 medium apple (150g)

1/4 cup (60ml) fresh lemon juice

300g frozen raspberries, thawed

250g strawberries, halved

2 cups (440g) sugar

Peel rind thinly from lemons, avoiding white pith. Cut rind into very thin strips. Peel and core apple, cut into thin wedges.

Combine rind, apple, juice, berries and sugar in large saucepan; stir over heat, without boiling, until sugar dissolves. Boil, uncovered, stirring occasionally, about 15 minutes or until jam jells when tested. Pour hot jam into hot sterilised jars; seal while hot.

MAKES about 3 cups (750ml)

Per tablespoon 0.1g fat; 223kJ

mandarin jelly

15 medium mandarins (3kg)

1 cup (250ml) fresh lemon juice

2 litres (8 cups) water

1.8kg (8 cups) sugar, approximately

Squeeze juice from mandarins, pour into large saucepan. Discard skins; chop mandarin flesh coarsely. Add mandarin flesh, lemon juice and the water to same pan; bring to a boil. Reduce heat; simmer, covered, 1 hour. Strain mixture through large piece of damp muslin into large bowl; allow mixture to drip through cloth for several hours or overnight. Do not squeeze or press the mixture through the cloth as this will result in cloudy jelly.

Measure the strained liquid, discard pulp. Allow correct amount of sugar (according to pectin test, page 3) to each cup of liquid. Return liquid with sugar to clean large saucepan; stir over heat, without boiling, until sugar dissolves. Boil, uncovered, without stirring, about 30 minutes or until jelly sets when tested. Pour hot jelly into hot sterilised jars; seal while hot.

MAKES about 1.25 litres (5 cups)

Per tablespoon 0.1g fat; 542kJ

36 pineapple jam

1 large pineapple (2kg), peeled, cored, chopped coarsely

1.25 litres (5 cups) water

2/3 cup (160ml) fresh lemon juice

1.3kg (6 cups) sugar

Combine pineapple, the water and juice in large saucepan; bring to a boil. Reduce heat; simmer, covered, about 1 hour or until pineapple is soft. Stir in sugar; stir over heat, without boiling, until sugar dissolves.
Boil, uncovered, without stirring, about 30 minutes or until jam jells when tested.
Pour hot jam into hot sterilised jars; seal while hot.

MAKES about 1.5 litres (6 cups)
Per tablespoon 0g fat; 314kJ

kiwi fruit jam

12 large (1.2kg) kiwi fruit

2 teaspoons citrus pectin

2 tablespoons water

2 tablespoons fresh lemon juice

2 cups (440g) sugar

green food colouring, optional

Cut peeled kiwi fruit into eighths, discard seeds and core. Blend or process pectin, the water, juice and 1 tablespoon of the sugar until smooth. Add kiwi fruit; process until chopped coarsely.

Combine kiwi fruit mixture with remaining sugar in large saucepan; stir over heat, without boiling, until sugar dissolves. Boil, uncovered, stirring occasionally, about 10 minutes or until jam jells when tested. Tint with colouring, if desired. Pour hot jam into hot sterilised jars; seal while hot.

MAKES about 2½ cups (625ml)

Per tablespoon 0.1g fat; 294kJ

38 peach and passionfruit jam

You will need about eight passionfruit for this recipe.

1 small orange (180g)

1 medium lemon (140g)

2 tablespoons water

2 cups (500ml) water, extra

7 medium peaches (1kg), peeled, sliced thinly

4 cups (880g) sugar, approximately

2/3 cup (160ml) passionfruit pulp

Chop unpeeled orange and lemon coarsely, remove and reserve seeds. Put seeds and the 2 tablespoons of water in small bowl; cover, set aside. Blend or process orange and lemon mixture until finely chopped. Combine fruit mixture with extra water in large bowl. Stand both fruit mixture and seeds, separately, overnight.

Drain seeds over small bowl; reserve liquid, discard seeds. Combine seed liquid with fruit mixture in large saucepan; bring to a boil. Reduce heat; simmer, covered, about 25 minutes or until rind is tender. Stir in peaches; simmer, covered, about 20 minutes or until peaches are soft.

Measure fruit mixture, allow 1 cup (220g) sugar to each cup of fruit mixture. Return fruit mixture with sugar to pan; stir over heat, without boiling, until sugar dissolves. Boil, uncovered, stirring occasionally, about 15 minutes or until jam jells when tested. Stand 5 minutes; stir in passionfruit pulp. Pour hot jam into hot sterilised jars; seal while hot.

MAKES about 1.25 litres (5 cups)

Per tablespoon 0g fat; 265kJ

Peach
&
Passionfruit

40 blueberry and passionfruit jam

You will need about two passionfruit for this recipe.

750g blueberries

3 cups (750ml) water

2½ cups (550g) sugar, approximately

¼ cup (60ml) fresh lemon juice

2 tablespoons passionfruit pulp

Combine blueberries and water in large saucepan; bring to a boil. Reduce heat; simmer, uncovered, about 20 minutes or until blueberries are tender. **Measure** fruit mixture, allow ¾ cup (165g) sugar to each cup of fruit mixture. Return fruit mixture with sugar and juice to pan; stir over heat, without boiling, until sugar dissolves. Boil, uncovered, stirring occasionally, about 20 minutes or until jam jells when tested. Stir in passionfruit pulp; stand 5 minutes. Pour hot jam into hot sterilised jars; seal while hot.

MAKES about 3 cups (750ml)

Per tablespoon 0g fat; 291kJ

dark **plum** jam

18 medium blood plums (2kg)

1 litre (4 cups) water

1/3 cup (80ml) fresh lemon juice

1.3kg (6 cups) sugar

Cut plums into quarters, remove stones. Combine plums and the water in large saucepan; bring to a boil. Reduce heat; simmer, covered, 1 hour. Add juice and sugar; stir over heat, without boiling, until sugar dissolves. **Boil**, uncovered, stirring occasionally, about 20 minutes or until jam jells when tested. Pour hot jam into hot sterilised jars; seal while hot.

MAKES about 2 litres (8 cups)

Per tablespoon 0g fat; 243kJ

42 mandarin and apricot jam

4 medium mandarins (800g)

1 medium lemon (140g)

1 2/3 cups (250g) dried apricots, chopped coarsely

1.25 litres (5 cups) water

1.5kg (7 cups) sugar, approximately

Peel rind from mandarins and lemon, taking care not to remove any white pith with the rind. Shred rind finely.
Discard membranes from mandarins and lemon; chop flesh coarsely, discarding seeds. Place rind, citrus flesh, apricots and the water in large saucepan; bring to a boil. Reduce heat; simmer, covered, about 45 minutes or until rind is transparent.
Measure fruit mixture, allow 1 cup (220g) sugar to each cup of fruit mixture. Return fruit mixture with sugar to pan; stir over heat, without boiling, until sugar dissolves. Boil, uncovered, stirring occasionally, about 10 minutes or until jam jells when tested. Pour hot jam into hot sterilised jars; seal while hot.

MAKES about 1.75 litres (7 cups)
Per tablespoon 0g fat; 327kJ

44 fresh **apricot** jam

20 (1kg) apricots

½ cup (125ml) water

¼ cup (60ml) fresh lemon juice

1kg (4½ cups) sugar

Halve apricots and remove stones. Combine apricots, the water and juice in large saucepan; bring to a boil. Reduce heat; simmer, covered, about 15 minutes or until apricots are tender. **Add** sugar; stir over heat, without boiling, until sugar dissolves. Boil, uncovered, stirring occasionally, about 30 minutes or until jam jells when tested. Stand 5 minutes. Pour hot jam into hot sterilised jars; seal while hot.

MAKES about 1.25 litres (5 cups)

Per tablespoon 0g fat; 290kJ

pawpaw and pineapple jam

2 medium firm pawpaws (2kg)

1 medium pineapple (1.25kg)

½ cup (100g) finely chopped glacé ginger

2 cups (500ml) fresh lemon juice

2kg (9 cups) sugar

Quarter, seed and peel pawpaws; chop into 2cm pieces. Peel pineapple, remove core; chop pineapple into 2cm pieces. Combine pawpaw, pineapple, ginger and juice in large saucepan; bring to a boil. Reduce heat; simmer, uncovered, 5 minutes.

Add sugar; stir over heat, without boiling, until sugar dissolves. Boil, uncovered, stirring occasionally, about 30 minutes or until jam jells when tested; stand 5 minutes. Pour hot jam into hot sterilised jars; seal while hot.

MAKES about 3 litres (12 cups)

Per tablespoon 0.1g fat; 1017kJ

46 honey sauternes jelly

5 large apples (1kg), chopped coarsely

2 tablespoons fresh lemon juice

2 cups (500ml) water

1 cup (250ml) sauternes

1/4 cup (60ml) honey

3 cups (660g) sugar, approximately

Combine apple (including seeds and cores), juice, the water, wine and honey in large saucepan; bring to a boil. Reduce heat; simmer, covered, 1 hour. Strain mixture through large piece of damp muslin into large bowl; allow mixture to drip through cloth for several hours or overnight. Do not squeeze or press the mixture through the cloth as this will result in cloudy jelly.

Measure the strained liquid, discard pulp. Allow the correct amount of sugar (according to pectin test, page 3) to each cup of liquid. Return liquid with sugar to clean large saucepan; stir over heat, without boiling, until sugar dissolves. Boil, uncovered, without stirring, about 10 minutes or until jelly sets when tested.

Pour hot jelly into hot sterilised jars; seal while hot.

MAKES about 3 cups (750ml)

Per tablespoon 0g fat; 413kJ

Chartreuse
ERNES
Contrôlée

48 lime ginger marmalade

6 large limes (600g)

1.5 litres (6 cups) water

1.5kg (7 cups) sugar, approximately

2 teaspoons grated fresh ginger

Slice unpeeled limes thinly, remove and discard seeds. Combine limes in large bowl with the water; cover, stand overnight.
Transfer lime mixture to large saucepan; bring to a boil. Reduce heat; simmer, covered, about 1 hour or until rind is tender.
Measure fruit mixture, allow 1 cup (220g) sugar to each cup of fruit mixture. Return fruit mixture with sugar to pan; stir over heat, without boiling, until sugar dissolves. Boil, uncovered, stirring occasionally, about 15 minutes or until marmalade jells when tested. Stir in ginger. Pour hot marmalade into hot sterilised jars; seal while hot.

MAKES about 2 litres (8 cups)
Per tablespoon 0g fat; 256kJ

black grape and port jelly

1kg black grapes

2 medium lemons (280g), chopped coarsely

1 litre (4 cups) water

½ cup (125ml) port

1kg (4½ cups) sugar, approximately

Combine grapes, lemon (including rind and seeds) and the water in large saucepan; bring to a boil. Reduce heat; simmer, covered, 45 minutes. Stir in port, crush grapes in pan using a potato masher. **Simmer**, covered, 45 minutes. Strain mixture through large piece of damp muslin into large bowl; allow mixture to drip through cloth for several hours or overnight. Do not squeeze or press the mixture through the cloth as this will result in cloudy jelly.

Measure the strained liquid, discard pulp. Allow the correct amount of sugar (according to pectin test, page 3) to each cup of liquid. Return liquid with sugar to clean large saucepan; stir over heat, without boiling, until sugar dissolves. Boil, uncovered, without stirring, about 15 minutes or until jelly sets when tested. Pour hot jelly into hot sterilised jars; seal while hot.

MAKES about 1 litre (4 cups)
Per tablespoon 0g fat; 411kJ

50 apricot rum conserve

$3\frac{1}{3}$ cups (500g) dried apricots

1 litre (4 cups) water

$\frac{1}{3}$ cup (80ml) fresh lemon juice

1kg ($4\frac{1}{2}$ cups) sugar

2 tablespoons dark rum

Combine apricots, the water and juice in large saucepan; bring to a boil. Reduce heat; simmer, covered, about 30 minutes or until apricots are tender.

Add sugar; stir over heat, without boiling, until sugar dissolves.

Boil, uncovered, stirring occasionally, about 15 minutes or until conserve jells when tested. Stir in rum. Pour hot conserve into hot sterilised jars; seal while hot.

MAKES about 1.5 litres (6 cups)

Per tablespoon 0g fat; 285kJ

52 lemon and passionfruit marmalade

You will need about six passionfruit for this recipe.

8 medium lemons (1.1kg)

2 litres (8 cups) water

1.3kg (6 cups) sugar, approximately

½ cup (125ml) passionfruit pulp

Remove rind thinly from lemons, avoiding white pith. Cut rind into thin strips. Remove and reserve pith from lemons, chop flesh coarsely; reserve seeds. Tie pith and seeds in piece of muslin. Combine rind, lemon flesh, muslin bag and the water in large saucepan; bring to a boil. Reduce heat; simmer, covered, about 1 hour or until rind is tender. Discard muslin bag. **Measure** fruit mixture, allow ¾ cup (165g) sugar to each cup of fruit mixture. Return fruit mixture with sugar to pan; stir over heat, without boiling, until sugar dissolves. Boil, uncovered, stirring occasionally, about 20 minutes or until marmalade jells when tested. Stir in passionfruit pulp; stand 5 minutes. Pour hot marmalade into hot sterilised jars; seal while hot.

MAKES about 2 litres (8 cups)
Per tablespoon 0g fat; 230kJ

thick-cut ginger, grapefruit and **orange** marmalade

2 medium grapefruit (850g)

2 medium oranges (480g)

1.75 litres (7 cups) water

1.5kg (7 cups) sugar, approximately

2 tablespoons grated fresh ginger

Cut fruit in half, remove and discard seeds. Cut fruit into quarters, then cut quarters into thick slices. Combine fruit with the water in large bowl; cover, refrigerate overnight.

Transfer fruit mixture to large saucepan; bring to a boil. Reduce heat; simmer, covered, about 45 minutes or until fruit is soft.

Measure fruit mixture, allow 1 cup (220g) sugar to each cup of fruit mixture. Return fruit mixture with sugar and ginger to pan; stir over heat, without boiling, until sugar dissolves. Boil, uncovered, stirring occasionally, about 40 minutes or until marmalade jells when tested. Pour hot marmalade into hot sterilised jars; seal while hot.

MAKES about 1.75 litres (7 cups)

Per tablespoon 0g fat; 306kJ

54 cumquat cointreau jam

1kg cumquats

1.5 litres (6 cups) water

1.5kg (7 cups) sugar, approximately

1/4 cup (60ml) Cointreau

Cut cumquats into quarters, remove and reserve seeds. Put seeds and 1 cup (250ml) of the water in small bowl; cover, set aside. Combine fruit with remaining water in large bowl. Stand both fruit mixture and seeds, separately, overnight.

Drain seeds over small bowl; reserve liquid, discard seeds. Combine fruit mixture and seed liquid in large saucepan; bring to a boil. Reduce heat; simmer, covered, about 45 minutes or until rind is tender.

Measure fruit mixture, allow 1 cup (220g) sugar to each cup of fruit mixture. Return fruit mixture with sugar to pan; stir over heat, without boiling, until sugar dissolves. Boil, uncovered, stirring occasionally, about 25 minutes or until jam jells when tested. Stand 5 minutes; stir in liqueur. Pour hot jam into hot sterilised jars; seal while hot.

MAKES about 1.5 litres (6 cups)

Per tablespoon 0g fat; 368kJ

56 blackberry jelly

1kg blackberries

2 cups (500ml) water

3 cups (660g) sugar, approximately

2/3 cup (160ml) fresh lemon juice

Combine berries and the water in large saucepan; bring to a boil. Reduce heat; simmer, covered, about 25 minutes or until berries are soft and pulpy. Strain mixture through large piece of damp muslin into large bowl; allow mixture to drip through cloth for several hours or overnight. Do not squeeze or press the mixture through the cloth as this will result in cloudy jelly.

Measure the strained liquid, discard pulp. Allow the correct amount of sugar (according to pectin test, page 3) to each cup of liquid. Return liquid with sugar and juice to clean large saucepan; stir over heat, without boiling, until sugar dissolves. Boil, uncovered, without stirring, about 20 minutes or until jelly sets when tested. Pour hot jelly into hot sterilised jars; seal while hot.

MAKES about 3 cups (750ml)

Per tablespoon 0.1g fat; 343kJ

redcurrant jelly

1.5kg redcurrants

1.5 litres (6 cups) water

1 teaspoon fresh lemon juice

2½ cups (550g) sugar, approximately

1 tablespoon Grand Marnier

Combine redcurrants, the water and juice in large saucepan; bring to a boil. Reduce heat; simmer, covered, about 30 minutes or until redcurrants are soft. Strain mixture through large piece of damp muslin into large bowl; allow mixture to drip through cloth for several hours or overnight. Do not squeeze or press the mixture through cloth as this will result in cloudy jelly.
Measure the strained liquid, discard pulp. Allow the correct amount of sugar (according to pectin test, page 3) to each cup of liquid. Return liquid with sugar to clean large saucepan; stir over heat, without boiling, until sugar dissolves. Boil, uncovered, without stirring, about 15 minutes or until jelly sets when tested. Stir in liqueur. Pour hot jelly into hot sterilised jars; seal while hot.

MAKES about 3 cups (750ml)
Per tablespoon 0.2g fat; 721kJ

58 strawberry liqueur conserve

250g strawberries

1 cup (220g) sugar

2 teaspoons finely grated lemon rind

2 tablespoons fresh lemon juice

liqueur

500g strawberries

1/2 cup (110g) sugar

1/2 cup (125ml) gin

Place strawberries in medium saucepan with sugar, rind, juice and reserved strawberries from liqueur. Stir gently over heat, without boiling, until sugar dissolves. Boil, uncovered, gently stirring, occasionally, about 10 minutes or until conserve sets to a spreading consistency when tested. Pour hot conserve into hot sterilised jars; seal while hot.

Liqueur Combine strawberries in jar with sugar and gin; cover, stand 3 days. Shake jar gently several times a day. Remove strawberries from liquid; reserve strawberries. (Liquid can be used as a dessert sauce or served as a liqueur).

MAKES about 2 cups (500ml)

Per tablespoon 0g fat; 293kJ

let's jam!

continued from page 3

Hints for success

- Select slightly under-ripe, unbruised, cleaned fruit.
- Use wide-topped aluminium, stainless-steel or enamel boilers or saucepans; do not use copper or unsealed cast-iron pans.
- Make sure the pan you use is big enough: a pan that's too small doesn't allow for the necessary evaporation and results in runny jam. As a guide, once the sugar has been added to the jam or jelly mixture in pan, the whole should not be any more than 5cm deep.
- An imbalance of acid and pectin also causes jam and jelly not to set. Lemon juice can be added and the mixture re-boiled until it jells. However, if the mixture has already darkened and tastes of caramel, it cannot be re-boiled. If it is still palatable, use commercial pectin (available in powdered form from some health food stores) to set the jam or jelly. Follow the directions on the packet.
- Use super-clean, just-sterilised jars.
- Stored correctly, your jams and jellies will keep for up to a year.

Sterilising, sealing and storage

Your storage jars must be glass and without chips or cracks. Just before use, they must be sterilised and dried, using clean hands and a clean tea-towel.

To sterilise jars, either...

1 Run the jars through the rinse cycle of your dishwasher, at the hottest water temperature. Do not use detergent.

2 Place cleaned jars on their sides in a large saucepan; cover with cold water. Cover pan and, over high heat, bring water to a boil; boil 20 minutes. Carefully remove jars from water; drain. Stand, top up, on wooden board. The heat from the jars will cause any remaining water to evaporate quickly.

3 Wash the jars in hot soapy water then rinse in clean hot water to remove soap. Stand jars, top up, on wooden board placed in cold oven (do not allow jars to touch); turn oven to very slow, leave for 30 minutes.

To seal jars

Special lined and treated or lacquered lids, available with home preserving outfits, are suitable for sealing; ordinary metal lids will corrode due to acid content of the preserve. Plastic screw-top lids also give a good seal. Wipe over sealed jars with clean tea-towel before labelling.

To store preserves

Store preserves in a cool, dark, dry place until required. If you live in a humid climate, the best storage place is your refrigerator. Once opened, all preserves must be covered and kept in the refrigerator.

glossary

amaretto an almond-flavoured liqueur.

blood plums sweet-flavoured fruit with deep-red flesh.

citrus pectin is available from health food stores.

coconut, flaked flaked and dried coconut flesh.

cointreau citrus-flavoured liqueur.

cumquat orange-coloured citrus fruit about the size of a walnut. Usually preserved or used for making jam, the skin is always retained.

food colourings available in liquid, powdered and concentrated paste forms.

ginger, glacé fresh ginger that has been crystallised in sugar syrup.

grand marnier orange-flavoured liqueur based on Cognac-brandy.

grapefruit large, yellow-skinned citrus fruit; has tart flavour.

jamsetta an Australian-made jam-setting mixture with pectin; it is available in 50g packets.

kiwi fruit also known as Chinese gooseberry.

liquid sweetener an artificial no-calorie sweetener; available from supermarkets.

orange, seville orange variety that is very tart in flavour; suitable only for jam-making.

passionfruit also known as granadilla; a small tropical fruit, native to Brazil, comprised of a tough skin surrounding edible black sweet-sour seeds.

pawpaw large tropical fruit with yellow-orange skin and flesh ranging from yellow to pink to orange in colour.

port sweet fortified wine with alcohol content of 18% to 20%.

redcurrant small, red berry.

rhubarb is a vegetable and only the firm, pinkish stems are eaten; leaves are toxic.

rosé wine: slightly sweet wine with pale-pink colour; made from dark grapes.

rum liquor made from fermented sugarcane.

sauternes a sweet white wine made from late-harvested premium grapes; often referred to as a botrytis or sticky wine.

sherry, sweet sweet fortified wine originally from the south of Spain.

sugar we used coarse, granulated table sugar, also known as crystal sugar, unless otherwise specified.

caster: also known as superfine or finely granulated table sugar.

tartaric acid is used in making sweets and preserves to prevent the crystallisation of the sugar.

tomato, green medium-sized green tomato that is excellent for frying or in relishes.

vinegar, white made from spirit of cane sugar.

whisky we used a good quality Scotch whisky.

wine, sweet white we used a moselle wine.

index

facts and figures 63

These conversions are approximate only, but the difference between an exact and the approximate conversion of various liquid and dry measures is minimal and will not affect your cooking results.

Measuring equipment

The difference between one country's measuring cups and another's is, at most, within a 2 or 3 teaspoon variance. (For the record, 1 Australian metric measuring cup holds approximately 250ml.) The most accurate way of measuring dry ingredients is to weigh them. For liquids, use a clear glass or plastic jug having metric markings.

Note: NZ, Canada, USA and UK all use 15ml tablespoons. Australian tablespoons measure 20ml.
All cup and spoon measurements are level.

How to measure

When using graduated measuring cups, shake dry ingredients loosely into the appropriate cup. Do not tap the cup on a bench or tightly pack the ingredients unless directed to do so. Level the top of measuring cups and measuring spoons with a knife. When measuring liquids, place a clear glass or plastic jug having metric markings on a flat surface to check accuracy at eye level.

Dry Measures

metric	imperial
15g	1/2oz
30g	1oz
60g	2oz
90g	3oz
125g	4oz (1/4lb)
155g	5oz
185g	6oz
220g	7oz
250g	8oz (1/2lb)
280g	9oz
315g	10oz
345g	11oz
375g	12oz (3/4lb)
410g	13oz
440g	14oz
470g	15oz
500g	16oz (1lb)
750g	24oz (1 1/2lb)
1kg	32oz (2lb)

We use large eggs having an average weight of 60g.

Liquid Measures

metric	imperial
30ml	1 fluid oz
60ml	2 fluid oz
100ml	3 fluid oz
125ml	4 fluid oz
150ml	5 fluid oz (1/4 pint/1 gill)
190ml	6 fluid oz
250ml (1cup)	8 fluid oz
300ml	10 fluid oz (1/2 pint)
500ml	16 fluid oz
600ml	20 fluid oz (1 pint)
1000ml (1litre)	1 3/4 pints

Helpful Measures

metric	imperial
3mm	1/8in
6mm	1/4in
1cm	1/2in
2cm	3/4in
2.5cm	1in
6cm	2 1/2in
8cm	3in
20cm	8in
23cm	9in
25cm	10in
30cm	12in (1ft)

Oven Temperatures

These oven temperatures are only a guide.
Always check the manufacturer's manual.

	°C (Celsius)	°F (Fahrenheit)	Gas Mark
Very slow	120	250	1
Slow	150	300	2
Moderately slow	160	325	3
Moderate	180 – 190	350 – 375	4
Moderately hot	200 – 210	400 – 425	5
Hot	220 – 230	450 – 475	6
Very hot	240 – 250	500 – 525	7

Food editor Pamela Clark
Associate food editor Karen Hammial
Assistant food editor Kathy McGarry
Assistant recipe editor Elizabeth Hooper

HOME LIBRARY STAFF
Editor-in-chief Mary Coleman
Managing editor (food) Susan Tomnay
Editor Julie Collard
Concept design Jackie Richards
Designer Caryl Wiggins
Book sales manager Jennifer McDonald
Group publisher Jill Baker
Publisher Sue Wannan
Chief executive officer John Alexander

Produced by *The Australian Women's Weekly* Home Library, Sydney.

Colour separations by ACP Colour Graphics Pty Ltd, Sydney.
Printing by Dai Nippon Printing, Korea

Published by ACP Publishing Pty Limited, 54 Park St, Sydney; GPO Box 4088, Sydney, NSW 1028. Ph: (02) 9282 8618 Fax: (02) 9267 9438.

awwhomelib@acp.com.au
www.awwbooks.com.au

Australia Distributed by Network Distribution Company, GPO Box 4088, Sydney, NSW 1028. Ph: (02) 9282 8777 Fax: (02) 9264 3278.

United Kingdom Distributed by Australian Consolidated Press (UK), Moulton Park Business Centre, Red House Road, Moulton Park, Northampton, NN3 6AQ. Ph: (01604) 497 531 Fax: (01604) 497 533 acpukltd@aol.com

Canada Distributed by Whitecap Books Ltd, 351 Lynn Ave, North Vancouver, BC, V7J 2C4, Ph: (604) 980 9852.

New Zealand Distributed by Netlink Distribution Company, Level 4, 23 Hargreaves St, College Hill, Auckland 1, Ph: (9) 302 7616.

South Africa Distributed by: PSD Promotions (Pty) Ltd, PO Box 1175, Isando 1600, SA, Ph: (011) 392 6065; and CNA Limited, Newsstand Division, PO Box 10799, Johannesburg 2000. Ph: (011) 491 7500.

Creative food: Jams and Jellies

Includes index.
ISBN 1 86396 231 X

1. Cookery (Jam). 2. Cookery (Jelly).
3. Fruit – Preservation.
I. Title: Australian Women's Weekly.
(Series: Australian Women's Weekly creative food mini series).
641.852

Cover: Whisky seville marmalade, page 22.
Stylist Vicki Liley
Photographer Mark O'Meara
Back cover: Lemon and coconut marmalade (left), page 13; Lime and fig marmalade (right), page 12.

The publishers would like to thank Country Road Homewares and The Bay Tree Kitchen Shop for props used in photography.

mini books